BMX Racing and Freestyle

Julie Nelson

Books

Raintree Steck-Vaughn Publishers

A Harcourt Company

Austin · New York
www.raintreesteckvaughn.com

Published by Raintree Steck-Vaughn Publishers, an imprint of Steck-Vaughn Company.

Library of Congress Cataloging-in-Publication Data
Nelson, Julie.
     BMX racing and freestyle/Julie Nelson.
          p. cm.-- (Extreme sports)
     Includes bibliographical references and index.
     ISBN 0-7398-4687-6
     1. Bicycle motocross--Juvenile literature [1.Bicycle motocross. 2. Stunt cycling. 3. Extreme sports] I. Title. II. Extreme sports (Austin, Tex.)

GV1049.3 N45 2001
796.6'2--dc21   2001019515

Printed and bound in the United States of America
1 2 3 4 5 6 7 8 9 10 WZ 05 04 03 02 01

Produced by Compass Books

Photo Acknowledgments
Tony Donaldson: title page, 4, 8-9, 12, 14, 18-19, 22, 24, 26-27, 29, 30, 32, 34, 36, 40, 42 top, 42 bottom, 43 top, 43 bottom; Unicorn/Jeff Greenberg: 10, 17; Unicorn/Les Van: Cover, 6

Content Consultants
Dan Quigley, Penn Cycle
Jerry Landrum, BMX Mania

Contents

BMX freestylers use their bikes to do tricks.

Introduction

BMX racing and freestyle are extreme sports that are growing more and more popular. BMXers ride bicycles on race courses and off of **ramps** and **obstacles** to do tricks. Extreme sports are relatively new sports taken up by daring athletes. Along with the fun of extreme sports, however, comes the risk of injury. People who participate in extreme sports must do everything they can to be safe.

You have probably heard of the X Games. But do you know what a **half-pipe** is? Do you know the difference between BMX racing and BMX freestyle? Who are the top BMXers in the word today? What do you need to do if you want to take up the sport? This book will answer these and many other questions.

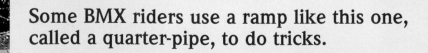
Some BMX riders use a ramp like this one, called a quarter-pipe, to do tricks.

How To Use This Book

This book is divided into parts called chapters. The title of the chapter tells you what it is about. The list of chapters and their page numbers appear in the Table of Contents on page 3. The Index on page 48 gives you page numbers where you can find important topics discussed in this book.

Each chapter has colorful photographs, captions, and side-bars. The photographs show you things written about in the book, so you will know what they look like. A caption is an explanation that tells you about the photograph. The captions in this book are in light blue boxes. Side-bars give you extra information about the subject.

You may not know what some of the words in this book mean. To learn new words, you look them up in a dictionary. This book has a dictionary called a glossary. Words that appear in boldface type are in the Glossary on page 44.

You can use the Internet sites listed on page 46 to learn more about topics discussed in this book. You can write letters to the addresses listed on page 46, asking them questions or to send you information.

BMX Racing and Freestyle

B MX stands for bicycle motocross. A BMX race is a bicycle race on a dirt track. The track contains many sharp turns, hills, and bumps.

BMX racers get to ride in mud and dirt. They ride standing up on their bikes. Sometimes there are crashes or wipe-outs.

This BMX rider has used a ramp to go
upside down at a competition.

Early BMX riders tried to imitate motorcycle riders on their bikes.

Freestyle

Another kind of bicycle riding is called freestyle. Freestyle riders do tricks with their bikes. They do not compete in races. Judges give them points for being good at tricks. They also get points for doing tricks that are different and difficult. In freestyle, the rider with the most points wins.

BMX and Freestyle Beginnings

BMX racing began in the early 1970s in California. Some young bike riders had the idea of using their bicycles to imitate motocross riders. Motocross is a kind of motorcycle dirt racing. A new sport was born.

Freestyle also started in the 1970s in California. Some young people had the idea of doing skateboarding tricks with their bicycles. Another new sport was born.

In 1976, a teenager named Bob Haro showed Bob Osborn some of the tricks he had invented. Osborn helped publish a magazine called *BMX Action*. Soon, Osborn began including pictures and articles about freestyle riding in his magazine. In a short time, kids in places other than California were trying the wild bicycle tricks.

All BMX riders will crash at some time. That is why they should wear helmets and protective equipment and clothing.

Getting Organized

By 1981, the International BMX Federation had begun to organize BMX racing around the world. In 1982, the first BMX championships were held in Daytona, Florida. Today, BMX and freestyle are more popular than ever. Millions of people watch them on television in the X Games on ESPN.

There are BMX races and freestyle competitions all over the world. It is especially popular in the United States and Europe, where people of all ages compete. In the United States, the American Bicycling Association (ABA) and the National Bicycle League (NBL) are the two most important BMX organizations. They can help young riders find clubs to join or places to practice. These also make rules for BMX and freestyle events.

BMX events are held year round. Each race starts with the riders standing on their bikes in a **starting gate**. The riders try to be the fastest out of the gate at the start of the race.

The leader of a race may use any part of the track. The other racers must get around the leader without crashing. Riders are allowed to touch each other, but they cannot crash on purpose. Riders who try dangerous things can be kicked out of the race or put into last place.

A BMX race is made up of three races called **motos**. One moto can take from 30 seconds to one minute to finish, and is one lap of the track. A moto is made up of as few as two riders and no more than eight riders at a time.

Points and Classes

Each rider is given points for the place where he or
she finishes. The top racer gets one point. At the end
of the three qualifying motos, the riders with the
fewest points race each other in a moto called a
main. After the main, the rider with the fewest points
is the overall champion.

There are many classes of BMX races. Riders are put into different groups based on age and skill level. The most experienced riders race each other. New riders are placed into their own motos.

BMX Tracks

A BMX race track can be inside or outside. Indoor tracks are good when the weather is bad. They also allow races to take place after dark. Indoor tracks are usually shorter than outdoor tracks and the races are quicker.

BMX tracks are made of mud, sand, and gravel. They can be 23 to 26 feet (7 to 7.9 m) wide at the start. Some tracks get as narrow 9 to 10 feet (2.7 to 3 m) in places.

Each race begins at a gate on top of a hill. The gate opens or drops to start the race. Riders must stay in their lanes during the first 50 feet (15 m).

Tracks contain many obstacles. These are difficult places to ride and they include hills, bumps, jumps, water, and sharp turns. Water and mud jumps are called hazards.

Some Hazards

There are many kinds of bumps and hills. High jumps can cause big crashes. **Whoop-de-dos**, or rhythm sections, are a series of several small hills. Riding over them is like riding on a roller coaster.

Tracks also have difficult turns. A **berm** is a fast turn with a high bank on the inside of the turn. A flat turn has no bank. Riders can fall more easily on flat turns. An **esse** is a turn that goes to the right and then to the left, like an "S."

The end of the race is called the **final stretch** or the last straighaway. It is usually a short distance of straight, flat track. The bikers race as fast as they can at the final stretch to see who wins.

What Is Freestyle Like?

There are freestyle competitions for one person, for two people riding together, and for teams of riders. Freestyle bikers can do ground tricks on flat surfaces called flatland. They also use street curbs or curved ramps to do jumps and other tricks.

Freestyle riders do many tricks using ramps. Most ramps are made of concrete or wood and are curved. They look like a pipe that has been cut in half or in

> ▲ **This BMX freestyler is doing an aerial.**

quarters. These ramps are called half-pipes and
quarter-pipes.

Riders ride up the ramp curves to do jumps called
aerials. They ride off the edge of the ramps and do
turns and flips in the air. Then they land again on the
ramp. A quarter-pipe is the most common BMX ramp.

Getting Started

Safety is an important part of becoming a good rider. Riders must wear safe equipment and clothing. They must protect their bodies. Riders can fall or crash at any time.

Helmets are the most important piece of safety equipment. They keep the head from being injured. Helmets also protect the ears and face. Most helmets have a visor that shields eyes from the sun. Riders should also wear mouth guards that are either built into their helmets or strapped onto them.

These riders at the X Games are wearing helmets to protect their heads.

What Safe BMX Riders Do

Safe riders wear long pants and a long-sleeved shirt. They wear pants that will not get stuck in the bike sprockets. They always wear shoes and socks when biking.

Safe riders always wear safety equipment. This includes a helmet, gloves, knee pads, and elbow pads.

If they fall, safe riders roll away from their bikes. They try to keep their arms and legs close to their bodies. They do this to avoid getting run over by other riders.

Safe riders take good care of their bikes. They check before every race to see that all the parts are working properly.

Safe riders never give other people a ride on their bikes.

Safe riders do not race or try tricks in the street. They only do these things at a track or in an area away from traffic.

Safe riders practice tricks and race skills only around other people, in case a rider gets injured. An injury is some kind of hurt or damage, such as broken bones or a sprain. A sprain means one of the body's joints has been twisted, tearing its muscles or ligaments. A ligament holds together the bones in a joint.

Safety Equipment

Several other parts of a rider's body should also be protected. Elbows and knees can get bumped and scraped. Padded BMX clothes called leathers protect riders. Extra pads for their knees and elbows are also available.

Riders should cover as much of their skin as possible. They should always wear long sleeved shirts and long pants. They should also wear gloves. Leather gloves help riders grip their bike handles better. They also protect their hands during a crash.

It is important that riders tuck their pant cuffs in or secure their pant cuffs. If cuffs are not secured, they can catch in the sprockets or spokes of a bike. Socks and shoes should always be worn. The shoes a rider wears should have good traction on the bottoms.

Rider Profile: Jill Kintner

Jill Kintner won many BMX titles in the NBL and ABA. Her favorite win was in the Junior Women's class at the World Championships. One of today's top pros, Kitner has advice for young people who want to ride. "Ride as much as you can, all the time," she says. "It's the best way to learn."

This freestyle bike was made especially for doing tricks.

The Bike

Early racers used their regular bikes to race. They fixed them up so they would race better. This was called "souping up" the bikes. Riders changed the bikes to make them stronger for racing. They wore football helmets and homemade padding to protect their bodies. Young people made their own dirt tracks in empty lots and fields.

A BMX bike is different from a street bike. It weighs less. It is also stronger. It has different kinds of tires and other parts than a regular bike. Most BMX bikes have 20-inch (50.8 cm) wheels. They weigh from 18 to 30 pounds (8.1 to 13.5 kg) and are designed to be easy to ride and steer.

The tires of BMX have knobs on them to help grab the dirt. BMX bikes are padded to protect the rider. The padding is soft so that the rider cannot get injured as easily in a crash.

Freestylers use different kinds of bikes than BMX racers. The freestyle bike must be strong and light to make it easier to do tricks.

This BMX racer is turning on a berm.

Freestyle Bikes

Freestyle bikes have handlebars and seats that can twist to help riders do tricks. The part that allows the handlebars to twist is called a rotor. There are also steps called platforms on the wheels, handlebars, and pedals. Riders stand on these platforms to do tricks. Freestyle bikes also have smoother tires. They all have brakes on the handlebars, and a few have brakes on the pedals as well. BMX bikes use only hand brakes.

Timeline

Early 1970s: Young people begin imitating motocross

1976: Freestyle begins

1979: *BMX Action* trick team tours the country

1981: International BMX Federation starts

1982: Daytona BMX Championships are held

Becoming a BMX Racer or Freestyle Rider

Almost anyone can become a BMX or freestyle rider if he or she is in good physical shape. Riders must have strong legs and healthy lungs.

Beginners must practice a long time before they can do freestyle tricks like this.

They can start when they are as young as age 3 or 4. World champion Jill Kitner began riding at age 8.

BMX racers study the track before a race. They learn all the obstacles and think about how to ride different parts of the race. Many riders even walk around the race track before a race. Every track is different.

The start is a big part of the race. Some say it is the hardest part. It is important because the rider who gets the best start has the lead. The leader can use any part of the track to keep the lead.

Racing Skils

Getting the "**holeshot**" means taking the lead out of the starting gate. The best way to win the holeshot is to work on timing at the gate. Riders try to move before the gate even opens, leaving just as it drops.

Riders sometimes use their feet and legs to push against the ground on sharp turns. Some experienced riders put out a foot to block other bikes from passing them. This can be dangerous, though, and should only be done by experienced riders.

Good riders can hit berms at high speeds. They learn how to not slow down. Riders who do not slow down in flat turns, however, can wipe out.

One place riders try to get around the leader is on the berms. This is called "berm warfare."

Rider Profile: Greg Hill

Greg Hill is one of the best known riders in BMX history. He started racing in 1977. He won all his races at the age of 14 and then turned pro. He was injured many times, but he always worked hard to come back. Many people think he is one of the best racers ever. He now speaks to groups about his racing career.

Flying high over big jumps looks daring. Riders
often crash when they land big jumps. Those who do
not crash usually land on the back wheel first. If a
rider lands on the front wheel first or on both wheels
at the same time, the rider will probably crash.

This is Dave Mirra doing a no-footer back flip to earn points from a judge at the X Games.

Smart Riders

Smart riders try not to fly too high on jumps. They lose too much time when they do. The race is not about who jumps highest, but is about who finishes the race fastest.

Riding Freestyle

Freestyle riding, though, is often about who can land the highest jumps and do the best tricks. In the kind of freestyle called mini or street, riders use benches, curbs, walls, and handrails to do tricks. These obstacles are found on or near streets. Sometimes small ramps are also used for tricks and jumps.

Flatriding freestyle is done without ramps or obstacles. Riders do different kinds of tricks, including spins and twirls.

Vert riding is a high flying form of freestyle. Riders use half-pipe and quarter-pipe ramps to catch big air. This allows them to do more difficult tricks. Another high flying form of freestyle riding is called dirt jumping. Dirt jumpers use dirt obstacles and ramps to catch air and do tricks.

This kind of aerial trick should only be attempted by experienced riders.

Learning Freestyle Skills

The best way to learn freestyle tricks is to practice with another rider. One person can hold the bike while the other person practices. This way tricks can also be done with less chance of falling.

Freestyle riders should not try to do too many things at once. They should first learn ground tricks such as **wheelies**. A wheelie is done by riding the bike with the front wheel off the ground. Another ground trick is a **kick turn**. A kick turn is done on a hill. The rider gets to the top of the hill and stops with the front wheel in the air. Then the rider twists the bike around to where it started and rides back down the hill.

Other ground tricks are **pogoing, sidewalking,** and endos. Pogoing is done by hopping on one tire. Sidewalking is done by hopping sideways. Endos are done by balancing a bike on only the front tire. If you fall over the front of your bike, that is also called an endo.

After learning ground tricks, riders can learn ramp tricks. Aerials are ramp tricks done on a bike in midair. The ramp is needed to get the bike and rider off the ground.

Sponsors are companies that put their names on riders' helmets and on their clothes.

Aerials

There are many kinds of aerial tricks. In a kick out, the rider throws the bike to the side in midair. In a **tabletop jump**, the rider lays the bike out flat in the air. Riders can also do aerial turns and endos.

Where to Train

BMX racers and freestylers can practice at many places. Many towns have BMX tracks. Certified tracks can be used for training, practice, or competition. Certified tracks are officially approved by BMX organizations. They are also BMX clubs people can join. The clubs **sponsor** races. Clubs also give information about other races around the country and the world.

Riders do not need a full track to train. They can use empty parking lots, gravel pits, empty pieces of land, woods, or open fields. Freestylers can practice at BMX tracks and at skateboard parks. They can also make their own ramps at home out of wood. They can try tricks on hills they find near driveways or in empty lots. Some freestylers even practice in empty swimming pools. Young riders should always practice with an adult watching.

It is important not to practice on streets or around cars. This can be dangerous. Riders and freestylers should always wear safety gear, even when practicing. It is safer to practice with other people around, in case somebody gets injured.

These riders are experienced at riding whoop-de-doos.

Who Are the Professional Riders?

Professional BMX and freestyle riders get paid to race, just like professional football players get paid to play football. A professional, or pro, is a person who gets paid to do what many people do just for fun. Riders must decide if they are good enough to turn pro. A rider who always wins all of his or her races might be ready to turn pro.

Professionals take good care of themselves and their bikes. They must train hard. They need to be in very good physical shape to race. They need strong legs and lungs. They cannot get tired in the middle of races.

In the United States, there are two professional BMX leagues—the American Bicycling Association (ABA) and the National Bicycling League (NBL).

Sponsors

A sponsor is a business or a person who pays for a rider or team to race. The sponsor pays for the bikes and also for safety equipment. Some sponsors pay for riders to travel to races around the country and the world.

Many sponsors are bike companies or shoe companies. Riders wear each sponsor's name on their leathers and on their bikes. Sponsors hope people will see their names and remember them.

Most riders never get sponsors. You do not need a sponsor to race. Only the top experts ever find sponsors who help them with expenses.

Rider Profile: David Mirra

Dave Mirra has 10 X Games BMX medals, more than anyone else. Eight of his medals are gold and two are silver. He started racing in 1981 and turned pro in 1987. His nickname is "Miracle Boy." He has won a medal in every event he's been in since 1995. He is famous for a double flip he did at the X Games.

Competing in
BMX and Freestyle

Hundreds of thousands of people ride in BMX races and freestyle events. BMX riders can start at an early age. More kids see BMX racing on TV and in person than ever before. They also read about BMX in books and magazines.

The sport of BMX has changed a lot since it began. The bikes get lighter and faster every year. The safety equipment also becomes better. The tracks are harder and more fun to ride on. BMX races are now held all over the world.

Did You Know?

Did you know that some BMX riders and fans have special ways of saying things? Whey they say "wired," they mean to do a trick right. When they say "amped," they mean to be excited. They call a helmet a "brain bucket" or a "lid." A rider who gets very dirty is called a "corndog." A wheel that gets bent badly is called a "potato chip."

Millions of people have watched Dave Mirra on television at the X Games BMX competitions.

X Games and Popularity

One of the most famous BMX events is called the X Games. These were begun by the sports television network ESPN in 1995 and were known as the Extreme Games. Today, this competition has become the best-known competition for all kinds of extreme sports.

Some people who make money from racing keep racing when they are in their 30s and 40s. They study the tracks they race. They learn what bikes are the best. They take good care of themselves and their equipment. It is the combined effort of people of all ages that makes BMX such a popular sport.

Rider Profile: Mat Hoffman

Mat Hoffman is known as "The Condor." He began racing in 1982 and turned pro two years later. In 2000, he came back from being injured. That year he finished first or second in every event he entered. Hoffman helped make freestyling well known to the world. He was the world champion from 1987 through 1996. He has his own business called Hoffman Bikes.

Quick Facts About
BMX Racing and

There were more than 60,000 members of the American Bicycle Association in 2000.

In the 1997 X-Games, Mat Hoffman won the gold medal for freestyle. He did it with three broken bones in his foot.

One of the most famous bike companies is Redline. It started in 1972, and all of its bikes are red and black.

Freestyler Bob Haro did some of his freestyle tricks in the movie *ET: The Extra-Terrestrial.*

Freestyle

The two most important groups for freestyle riders are the American Freestyle Association and the National Freestyle Association.

The BMX world record for the 50-yard (45.5 m) dash is held by Brian Lopes, who raced that distance in 4.78 seconds.

Glossary

aerial (AIR-ee-uhl)—a trick done in midair with the help of a ramp

berm (BURM)—a banked turn

esse (ESS)—a turn on the track that curves both ways

final stretch (FYE-nuhl STRECH)—the straight run at the end of a race

half-pipe (HAF PIPE)—a U-shaped jump with two curved walls

helmet (HEL-mit)—a hard kind of hat that protects a person's head

holeshot (HOHL-shot)—to grab an early lead out of the gate

kick turn (KIK-turn)—a trick where the rider turns around at the top of the ramp

main (MAYN)—the final race of an event to determine the champion

moto (MOH-toh)—one lap or one race on a track

obstacle (OB-stuh-kuhl)—something that makes a track more difficult to ride

pogoing (poh-GOH-ing)—to hop on one tire

professional (pruh-FESH-uh-nuhl)—a person who makes money doing something others do for fun

quarter-pipe (KWOR-tur PIPE)—a curved ramp used to get high for aerials

ramp (RAMP)—a curved surface used for freestyle tricks

sidewalking (SIDE-wawk-ing)—to hop sideways on a bike

sponsor (SPON-sur)—a company who pays someone to use or advertise its product

starting gate (START-ing GAYT)—the area at the front of the race where riders begin

tabletop jump (TAY-buhl-top JUHMP)—a trick where the rider lays the bike flat in the air

wheelie (WEE-lee)—to ride on only the back tire

whoop-de-dos (WOOP-dee-doos)—many bumps close together on a track

Internet Sites and Addresses

American Bicycle Association BMX
http://www.ababmx.com

BMXmania.com
http://www.bmxmania.com

BMXWEB.COM
http://bmxweb.com/home.cfm

BMX Non Stop!
http://bmxnonstop.com/bmx/index.html

EXPN.Com BMX Index
http://expn.go.com/bmx/index.html

Girls Race BMX
http://girlsracebmx.com

National Bicycle Association
http://www.nbl.org

ROOST BMX
http://www.roostbmx.com

American Bicycle Association
P.O. Box 718
Chandler, AZ 85244

National Bicycle League
P.O. Box 729
Dublin, OH 43017

Snap Magazine
P.O. Box 469020
Escondido, CA 92046-9664

Books to Read

Brimner, Larry Dane. *BMX Freestyle.* New York: Franklin Watts, 1987. This book is an introduction to performing stunts and routines on motocross bicycles with instructions for tricks and advice on equipment, safety, and competitions.

Haro, Bob. *Freestyle Moves.* Haro Designs, 1982. This book discusses and teaches about simple and complex tricks for riders of BMX bikes.

Jay, Michael. *BMX Bikes.* New York: Franklin Watts, 1985. This book describes a bicycle motocross race and discusses bike design, stunt riding, and safety tips.

Osborn, Bob. *The Complete Book of BMX.* Harper and Row, 1984. This book, written by a pioneer of BMX publishing, discusses many different aspects of the sport of BMX bicycle riding.

Index